IT'S BRITNEY...!

IT'S BRITNEY...!

IT'S BRITNEY...!

IT'S BRITNEY...!

50 REASONS SHE'S OUR

FOREVER QUEEN

IT'S BRITNEY...!

Smith Street Books

IT'S BRITNEY...!

BILLIE OLIVER AND STEPHANIE SPARTELS

EVERYONE KNEW BRITNEY WOULD BECOME A **MEGASTAR.** FROM THE AGE OF TWO, SHE'D CLAIM THE FAMILY BATHROOM TO **SING INTO**

PRESS FOR *Champagne*

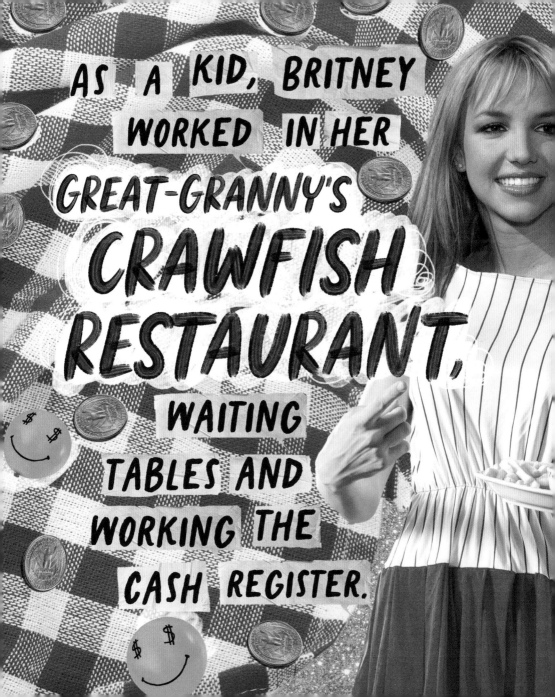

AS A KID, BRITNEY WORKED IN HER GREAT-GRANNY'S **CRAWFISH RESTAURANT**, WAITING TABLES AND WORKING THE CASH REGISTER.

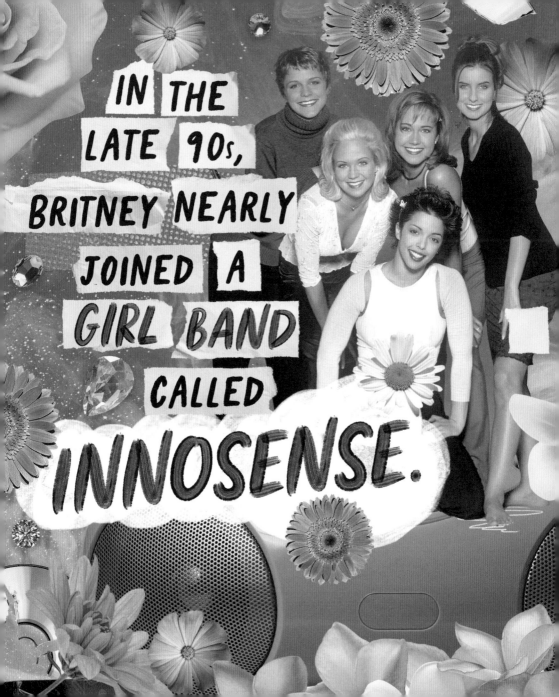

IN THE LATE 90s, BRITNEY NEARLY JOINED A GIRL BAND CALLED INNOSENSE.

THANKFULLY FOR ALL OF US, SHE WENT SOLO.

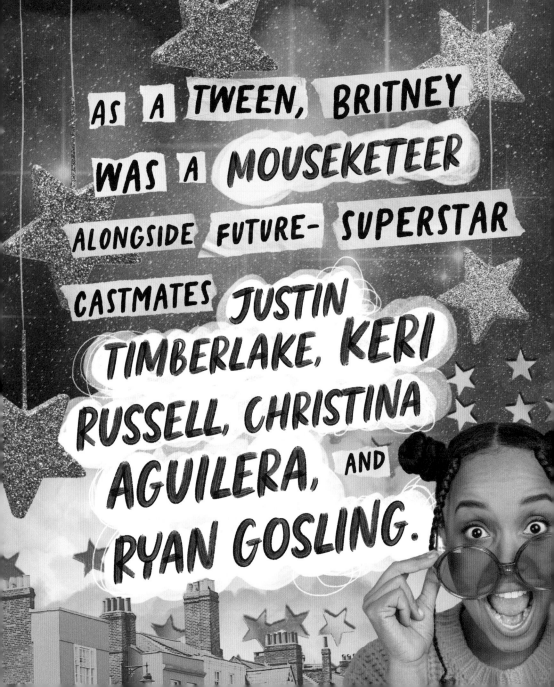

AS A TWEEN, BRITNEY WAS A MOUSEKETEER ALONGSIDE FUTURE-SUPERSTAR CASTMATES JUSTIN TIMBERLAKE, KERI RUSSELL, CHRISTINA AGUILERA, AND RYAN GOSLING.

WHEN THE MICKEY-MOUSE CLUB ENDED, SPEARS MOVED BACK TO MISSISSIPPI AND SPENT SOME TIME AS THE POINT GUARD ON HER HIGH SCHOOL'S BASKETBALL TEAM.

SHE WAS SUCCEEDED BY A YOUNG NATALIE PORTMAN.

BEFORE BRITNEY HAD EVEN RELEASED HER DEBUT RECORD, SHE PERFORMED AT MALLS ACROSS THE US

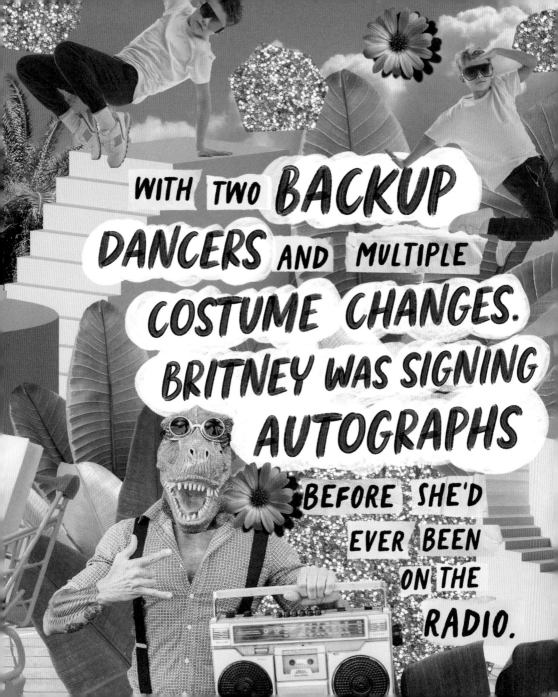

WITH TWO **BACKUP DANCERS** AND MULTIPLE **COSTUME CHANGES. BRITNEY WAS SIGNING AUTOGRAPHS** BEFORE SHE'D EVER BEEN ON THE RADIO.

WE HAVE **BRITNEY** TO THANK FOR THE RETURN OF **TEEN POP** IN THE 90s.

WHEN **BRITNEY** WAS FIRST GETTING TRACTION, SHE'D REPLY TO EACH FAN EMAIL *HERSELF.*

*CRYING
FACE EMOJI*

WHICH MIGHT EXPLAIN HER ADVENTUROUS AND BUSINESS-SAVVY WAYS.

SHE AUDITIONED FOR **THE NOTEBOOK**

AND WE'D DIE TO SEE THAT REMAKE.

IN 1999,

'... BABY ONE

MORE TIME'

WAS THE

MOST REQUESTED

MUSIC VIDEO

ON MTV.

IT SHOULD'VE WON THE OSCAR FOR **BEST PICTURE,** TOO.

SHE WAS A JUDGE FOR A SEASON OF THE X-FACTOR, WHICH IS ONLY FITTING. WHO HAS 'IT' MORE THAN THE QUEEN OF POP?

SHE HAS TRANSFORMED WHAT IT MEANS TO HAVE A *VEGAS RESIDENCY.*

WAS ALL BRITNEY'S IDEA.

SHE'S A HIGHLY
TRAINED GYMNAST.
SEND BRITNEY TO THE
PARIS 2024 OLYMPICS,
PLEASE.

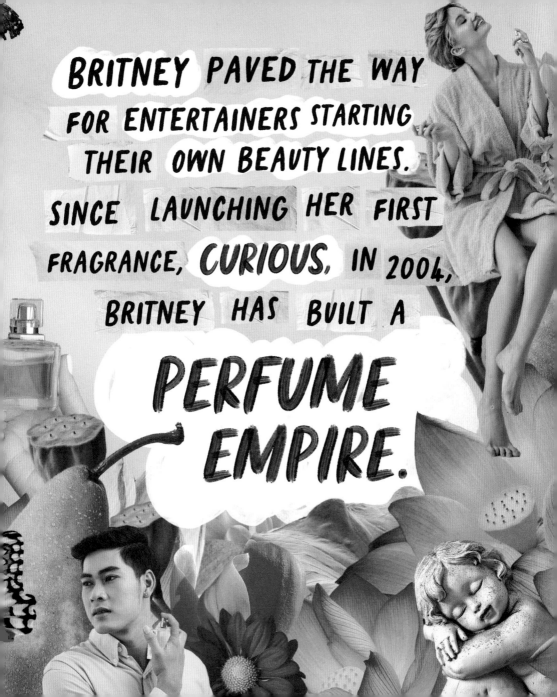

BRITNEY PAVED THE WAY FOR ENTERTAINERS STARTING THEIR OWN BEAUTY LINES. SINCE LAUNCHING HER FIRST FRAGRANCE, CURIOUS, IN 2004, BRITNEY HAS BUILT A

PERFUME EMPIRE.

WHEN THINGS IN BRITNEY'S LIFE WERE AT THEIR MOST **CHAOTIC,**

SHE WAS STILL CREATING MUSIC THAT CHANGED THE WORLD.

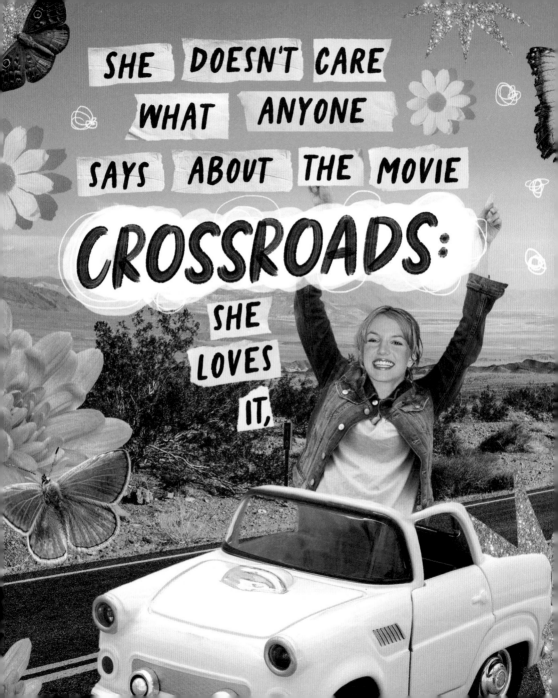

SHE DOESN'T CARE WHAT ANYONE SAYS ABOUT THE MOVIE CROSSROADS: SHE LOVES IT.

BRITNEY KNOWS HOW TO DELIVER A **PER**

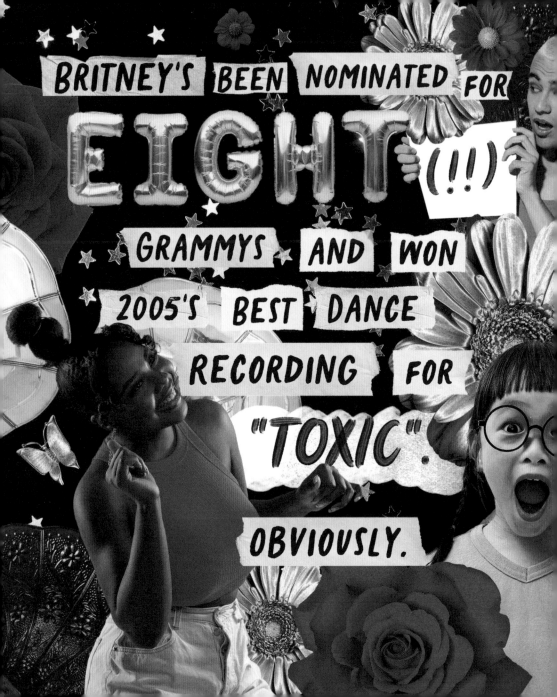

BRITNEY'S BEEN NOMINATED FOR

EIGHT (!!)

GRAMMYS AND WON 2005'S BEST DANCE RECORDING FOR "TOXIC". OBVIOUSLY.

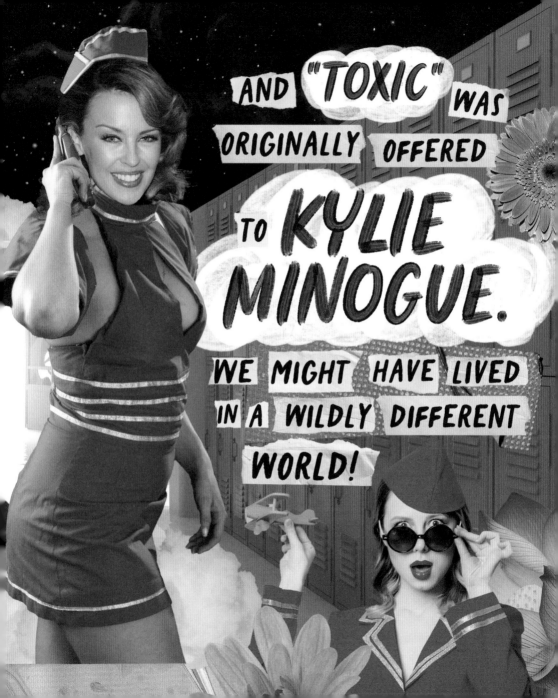

AND "TOXIC" WAS ORIGINALLY OFFERED TO KYLIE MINOGUE. WE MIGHT HAVE LIVED IN A WILDLY DIFFERENT WORLD!

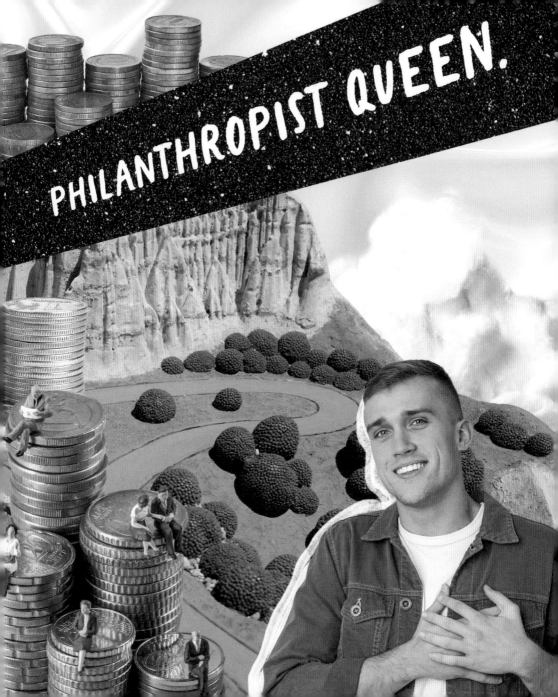

PHILANTHROPIST QUEEN.

BY HER THIRD STUDIO ALBUM, BRITNEY WAS WRITING HER OWN MATERIAL. SHE KEPT TRACK OF HER MELODIES AND LYRICS BY CALLING HER HOME PHONE TO LEAVE HERSELF A MESSAGE.

BRITNEY DOES MORE THAN SING AND DANCE. WITH LATER ALBUMS, BRITNEY *CO-PRODUCED* HER OWN MATERIAL AND ASSUMED CREATIVE CONTROL OF HER *POP EMPIRE.*

SHE LED THE
PINK POM-POM
HAIR
REVOLUTION
OF THE
2000s.

BRITNEY HAS NEVER LET ANYONE SHAME HER OUT OF

WEARING WHAT SHE WANTS.

"I THINK THE BODY'S A **BEAUTIFUL THING,** AND YOU SHOULD NOT HIDE YOURSELF. IF YOU FEEL LIKE WEARING SOMETHING THAT MAKES YOU FEEL GOOD ABOUT YOU...

I SAY, "GO FOR IT."

BRITNEY HAS THE MOST DEDICATED FANBASE OF ANY POP ICON. THROUGHOUT THE #FREEBRITNEY MOVEMENT, THEY FOUGHT TO SHED LIGHT ON HER CONSERVATORSHIP.

SHE APPRECIATES THE FINER THINGS IN LIFE, LIKE FUDGE.

AND
CHILI
DOGS.

WHEN SHE'S NOT BUSY MAKING SMASH HITS, BRITNEY LOVES TO READ A BIT OF

DANIELLE

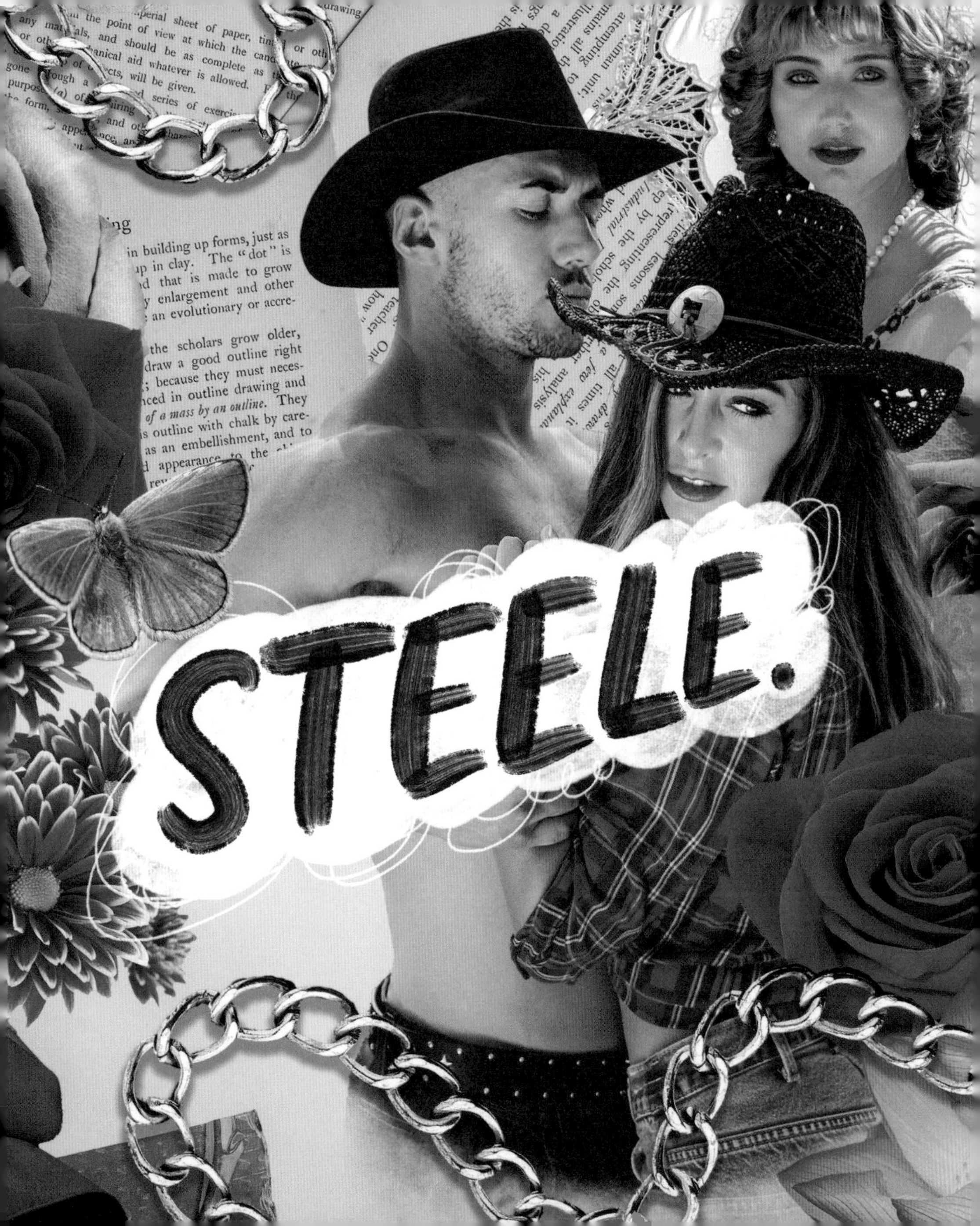
STEELE.

BRITNEY **REFUSES** TO STOP A SHOW FOR A MERE **WARDROBE MALFUNCTION.** INSTEAD, SHE FINISHES HER NUMBERS WITHOUT MISSING A BEAT.

BRITNEY'S HAD CAMEOS ON MANY TV SHOWS.

CAN A STUDIO EXEC OFFER HER A *LEAD ROLE* ASAP? TYVM.

BRITNEY WANTS **NATALIE PORTMAN** TO PLAY HER IN THE MOVIE VERSION OF HER LIFE,

AND WE WOULD 100% CROWDFUND THAT FILM RIGHT NOW.

BRITNEY PROVIDED THE BLUEPRINT FOR THE GREATEST POP STARS OF THE 21ST CENTURY. LADY GAGA SAID BRITNEY

"TAUGHT US ALL HOW TO BE FEARLESS, AND THE INDUSTRY WOULDN'T BE THE SAME WITHOUT HER."

NICKI MINAJ SAID

"THE FACT THAT SHE CAME BACK OUT WITH JUST SO MUCH FIRE INSPIRES ME, AND IT INSPIRES YOUNG WOMEN AND PEOPLE ALL OVER THE WORLD."

BRITNEY APPEARED AT THE 2001 SUPER BOWL HALFTIME SHOW, JOINING MARY J. BLIGE AND NELLY TO FEATURE IN NSYNC AND AEROSMITH'S FINALE.

LEGENDS ONLY!

THIS SHOULD BE CELEBRATED THE WORLD OVER.

ALMOST ANYONE WHO HEARS THE FIRST BARS OF "TOXIC" KNOWS THAT THEIR NIGHT IS ABOUT TO ESCALATE.

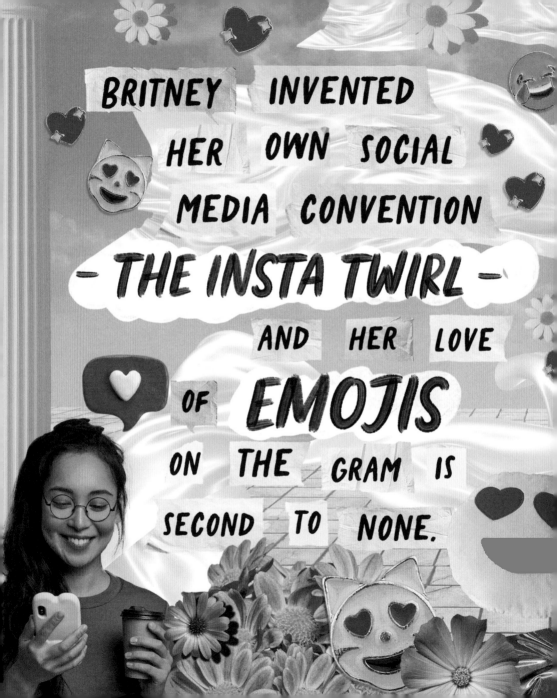

FOLLOWING SCRUTINY — AND DOWNRIGHT CRUELTY — FROM THE **PAPARAZZI** AND **TABLOID MEDIA,** BRITNEY HAS RECLAIMED HER STORY AND FORCED US TO REFLECT ON WHAT WE ASK OF YOUNG, FAMOUS WOMEN.

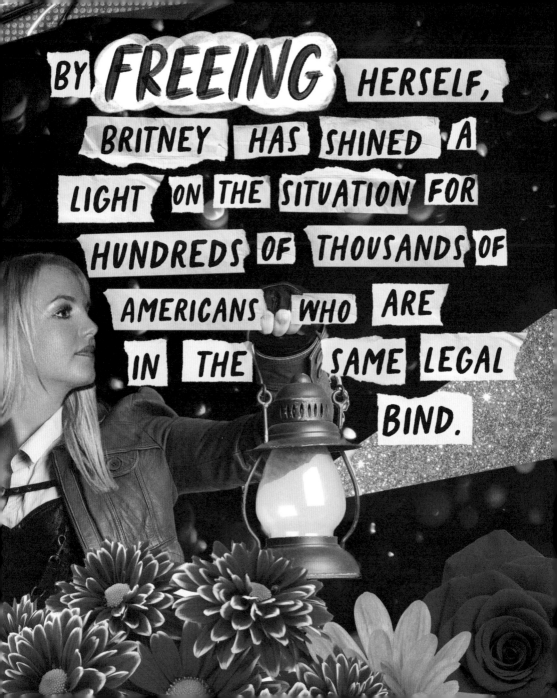

BRITNEY IS EMBARKING ON A NEW JOURNEY WITH HER PARTNER, SAM ASGHARI.

OUR HEARTS ARE TRULY MELTING FOR THEM.

BRITNEY

DID, IN FACT, GET TO WORK TO BECOME AN ABSOLUTE STAR, AND HAS EARNED HER PLACE IN OUR HEARTS.

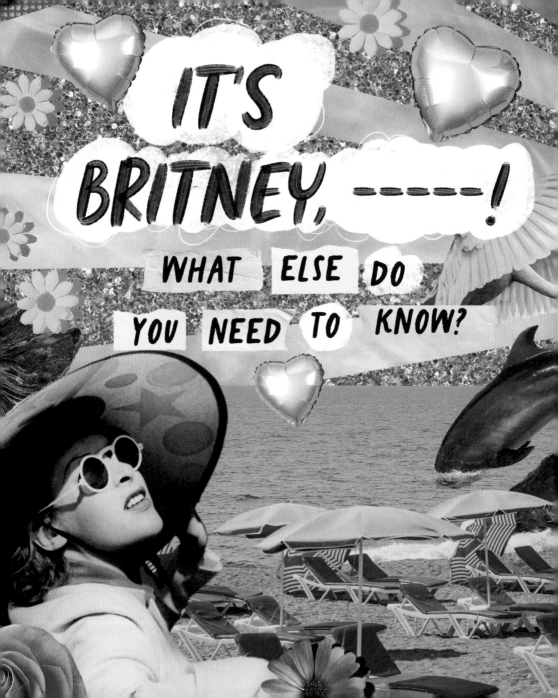

Smith Street Books

Published in 2022 by Smith Street Books
Naarm | Melbourne | Australia
smithstreetbooks.com

ISBN: 978-192275-401-1   Urban Outfitters: 978-1-92275-411-0

Cover photograph © Kevin Mazur/WireImage/Getty Images
Copyright stock photography © shutterstock.com, stock.adobe.com, alamy.com & unsplash.com

Publisher: Paul McNally
Project editor: Avery Hayes & Patrick Boyle
Design and layout: Stephanie Spartels
Proofreader: Hannah Koelmeyer

Printed & bound in China by C&C Offset Printing Co., Ltd.

Book 234

10 9 8 7 6 5 4 3 2 1

Please note: This title is not affiliated with or endorsed in any way by Britney. We are just big fans. Please don't sue us.